Ruby's

Written by Rosalind Malam
Illustrated by Jennifer Cooper

Harcourt Achieve

Rigby • Saxon • Steck-Vaughn

www.HarcourtAchieve.com
1.800.531.5015

Last summer I went to live with Dad. My old dog Skipper came, too. But soon after that, Skipper died. He'd been my friend as long as I could remember, and I was sure I'd never love another dog.

One afternoon, I was in the yard when I saw a strange dog.

"Hey, Dad!" I yelled. "There's a dog in our yard!"

Dad came to look. The dog had white feet and a stumpy tail that nearly wagged itself right off when she saw us.

"Where did she come from?" asked Dad. "Put Skipper's leash on her. We have to find out where she belongs."

We asked everywhere, but no one owned the dog. No one had even seen her before.

"Good," I said. "We can keep her! Let's call her Ruby."

"I'm sure the dog has a name of her own," said Dad. "And I'm sure she does have owners and that they'll be missing her."

Ruby crept up to the table and looked at my plate."The only thing **she's** missing right now is dinner!" I laughed.

We put ads in the local paper, but nobody answered them. Ruby stuck to me like bubble gum. We played games and went exploring together. Ruby loved the beach more than anything.

She always knew how to get our attention. When Nana Hawkins came to visit, Ruby charged around the room with a pair of Dad's underwear! She just knew Nana didn't like dogs inside.

If we worked in the yard, there was Ruby, poking her nose into everything. Once she pounced on a rosebush Dad was about to plant . . . then before you could say "jumping jelly beans", she'd bounded away with the hose!

One day Dad noticed that Ruby was looking fatter. "You've been giving her too much junk food," he told me.

But I'd noticed something, too — how often Ruby sat staring out the window, as if she was waiting for someone.

I didn't want to think about it.

Over the holidays, Dad said we could visit Aunt Rosie. It took four hours to get there, so we left home early. We were almost there when Dad asked if I'd remembered to pack Ruby's food. I hadn't, so we stopped at a pet store.

It was Dad who saw the photo stuck to the pet store window. It was a photo of a dog with white feet. It was definitely Ruby. Under the photo, in big red letters, a notice said:

MISSING, ALLIE

A phone number was included.

I just couldn't stop crying. I begged Dad not to make the phone call. He hugged me tight and said, "Remember when you first came to stay with me, and Skipper disappeared? And how you felt when he was returned the next day?"

I remembered . . . there are some things you never forget!

It was the hardest thing I'd ever done, letting Ruby go home. When Dad took her back, he wanted me to come, too. I couldn't do it. Ruby put her chin on my shoulder as I whispered goodbye. She couldn't understand why I was so sad.

How Ruby came to us will always be a mystery, but time really dragged when she left us.

Then one night, the telephone rang. Dad went to answer it and came back looking excited.

"That was Mr. Miles, Ruby's owner. He wants us to visit and says he has a surprise for you."

"You mean he's giving Ruby back to me?"

Dad looked at me sadly. "No. Ruby's back where she belongs. But she'd love to see you again. Are you ready to see her, too?"

Of course I wanted to see Ruby, but it would make me sad all over again.

Dad put his arm around me. "Perhaps it's time to get another dog — one of your very own."

"Have another dog? After Ruby? Never!"

Dad smiled. He'd heard those words before."Did loving Ruby make you love Skipper less?" he asked.

I thought about it. Loving Ruby hadn't changed the way I felt about Skipper. He has a special place in my heart that no one else could fill. But Ruby has her special place, too, and nothing will ever take that away.

So Dad and I went to Mr. Miles' place. Mr. Miles seemed really happy to see me.

"I can't thank you enough for taking care of my dog," he said. "It was lonely without her. Your Dad thought that junk food had made her fat, but . . . follow me!"

He led us around the back of his house to a shed.

There was Ruby, lying inside a large wooden box. She wagged her stumpy tail and whined. She seemed happy to see me, but she didn't get up. I could hardly believe my eyes when I saw the reason why! Three little puppies were snuggled beside her, fast asleep.

"That little red one looks like her mother," Mr. Miles was saying. "But the striped one — he's a real clown! Take your pick."

So everything turned out well in the end. I had my very own puppy. We love each other, and he comes with me everywhere. And every vacation we all go back to see Mr. Miles and Ruby.

Recounts

Recounts tell about something that has happened.

A recount tells the reader

- what happened

- to whom

- where it happened

- when it happened

A recount tells events in sequence . . .

. . . and has a conclusion.

19

Guide Notes

Title: Ruby's Secret
Stage: Fluency (4)

Text Form: Recount
Approach: Guided Reading
Processes: Thinking Critically, Exploring Language, Processing Information
Written and Visual Focus: Text Highlights

THINKING CRITICALLY
(sample questions)

- What do you think this story could be about? Look at the title and discuss.
- Look at the cover. How do you know that the girl and her father like animals?
- Look at pages 2 and 3. What sort of person do you think the narrator is? Why do you think that?
- Look at pages 4 and 5. What do you think the narrator and her dad did to try and find Ruby's owner?
- Look at pages 10 and 11. How do you think Ruby's owner felt when he heard that she had been found?
- Look at pages 12 and 13. Why do you think the narrator said that seeing Ruby would *make me sad all over again*?

EXPLORING LANGUAGE

Terminology
Spread, author and illustrator credits, imprint information, ISBN number

Vocabulary
Clarify: stumpy, bounded, charged, whined
Adjectives: *white* feet, *stumpy* tail, *junk* food
Pronouns: I, he, she, her, us
Homonyms: died/dyed, tail/tale, no/know, one/won
Antonyms: answered/ignored, special/ordinary, forget/remember
Synonyms: surprise/shock, special/extraordinary, excited/happy

Print Conventions
Apostrophes – possessive (Ruby's secret, Skipper's leash), ellipses, dashes